In Times of Joy

THE COMPLETE POEMS OF JOY DOOLAN

Joy Doolan

With Forward by T C Wynstead

Published by Storixus Publishing and Media
Mossman, Australia

© 1992 Joy Doolan
Forward © 2022 T C Wynstead

All rights reserved. This book or parts thereof may not be reproduced in any form, stored in any retrieval system, or transmitted in any form by any means — electronic, mechanical, photocopy, recording, or otherwise — without prior written permission of the publisher, except as provided by United States of America copyright law and fair use.

ISBN 978-0-6483640-9-2

www.storixus.com

In Memory of
Joy Doolan

Died 4-1-2007
Aged 77

Beloved wife to Raymond

"Another day gone by; another night
Creepin' along to douse Day's golden light;
Another dawning when the night is gone,
To live an' love - an' so life mooches on."
   - The Mooch O' Life, from The Songs of a
   Sentimental Bloke, C. J. Dennis

Table of Content

Joy and Laughter	1
The colours of my world	2
For Ray	3
A loving touch	5
How?	6
Destiny	7
Times past	8
Love lost	9
I think of you	10
To a friend	11
Childhood	12
To dream dreams	14
Harmony	15
My friend James	16
Thirteen	17
The Drover	18
Remember?	20
Greetings from across the sea	22
Have no regrets	24
The carousel	26
My song of joy	27
Vale Hal	28
The rainbow	29
The spirit of delight	30
Perchance to dream	31
Northern beauty	32
Peace on earth	33
Round the crib	34
The dignity of labour	35
The dying year	36
The Visit	38
Life: a celebration	39
Good Friday	40
Night song	41
A friend	42
The harvest	543

Daughter of Chernobyl	44
A coat of many colours	45
A bunch of flowers	46
A dead dream	47
Long ago	48
When hope dies	50
When love is born	51
The quiet time	52
Perfect peace	53
Now	54
Recession	55
Gone	57
Wonder	58
The seasons change	60
Waiting	61
Early Memories	62
Today	64
The land that time forgot	65
Thank you	66
The worst of times	67
The best of times	69
The sun goes down	70
The dancing air	71
Whispers on the wind	72
I like trains	73
Winter of despair	74
The spring of hope	75
A sign of the times	76
Ever after	77
The grave	78
Young love	79
Last days on Magnetic Island	80
When twilight goes	82
Gold	83
Winter's end	84
Looking back	85
A land for all seasons	86
Wild horses	87

Brief encounter	88
Cane country	90
Southland in autumn	92
New Ideas	93
The old soldier	94
Impermanence	95
The old man	97
The darkest night	98
The faded lady	99
Abandoned	100
I did not want to know	101
Arms	102
An imperfect world	103
From a hospital bed	105
Cat's meat	107
I love	108
Melbourne seasons	109
Youth and age	112
The cormorants	113
Cry havoc	114
A beautiful world	115
Collateral damage	116
Desert Storm	118
The war is over	119
Shame	120
One small child	121
Why?	122

Forward

Joy Doolan is one of the great unknown poets and talents of Australia. I was fortunate enough to be with her throughout the journey that has culminated in the collection of poems contained in this book. A journey that started with a submission of her first poem to the late-night talk back radio show called *Aussies on the Line*, on 3UZ in Melbourne.

This poem, and subsequent ones were well received for the shows poetry segment which showcased original poetry from the show's listeners. Buoyed by the positive feedback from her fellow insomniacs and shift workers Joy continued to write. Several her pieces were selected to be included in a book of verse called *The Poet in Us All*, which contained a selection of poetry from the show's listeners.

Joy published two of her own collections of works, *Joy and Laughter*, and *Life's like That*, both in 1992. At this time the show *Aussies on the Line*, one of Joy's key motivations for writing, was going through significant changes as the station progressively adopted and Sport and Racing program. Although Joy did continue to write poetry after her books were published, none of this poetry has survived. It was also during this time that Joys health started to have an impact on her daily life, her lungs started to fail. It was not long before she needed to keep an oxygen tank on hand.

The poetry that Joy created is raw and honest. Joy had a hard life at times, and she translated these times to the page, along with the good times. In her poems we can all find ourselves and relate to the emotions that she openly shares. To read her poetry is to travel along with her, as she discovers a deeper meaning in actions of everyday life.

In the darkest times, Joy remained positive and cared abundantly for those around her. It is this aspect of her life that was most imbued in her poetry. This is also the greatest gift which she gave to me, along with her teachings on poetry. Without her caring nature and the time she spent with me to educate me on English; to not just understand words, but to see the deeper meaning behind them and the power of how to use them, I would today not be able to call myself a poet.

Joy was heavily influence by turn of the contrary Australian poets, particularly Henry Lawson and C. J. Dennis. Her style however, is hers alone, and the feel of her poetry captures the ebbs and flows of life, the struggles, the loss and the abundance of happiness. Her poetry reflects sensitivity and caring, which is a good description of the way Joy lived her life.

Thank you Joy, for all the gifts you have bestowed on me, and for the lessons that continue to be shared through your words.

T.C. Wynstead.
Friends and Poet

Joy and Laughter

Joy and laughter rule the day
while sadness looks the other way.
If we could all but seize the time
and hold it close with hope sublime
till love appears with laughing face
and empty dreams of old replace.
The shadows in your eyes dissolve
you hold the world with new resolve
chasing other people's tears
with heart and mind, that knows no fears.
The seasons leave all grief behind
the landscape of the heart I find
shining brightly in the noonday sun
a season of mirth now just begun.
The thousand sorrows past are gone
and you and I, we now are one.
The emptiness of former years
is gone and with it wasted tears.

The Colours of My World

If I could weave the colours of the landscape
    into my heart with spools of silken thread
If I could capture from the misty hills of morning
    the smoky fog of steamy mountain bed
If I could see in daylight's dying hours
    the rustic reds and pinks and mauves so pale
If I could gather from the dew-laden grasses
    the sparkling gems that fall likes summer hail
I wonder could I hold these wondrous colours
    deep in my mind's eye, never lost to be
I wonder could I see them just as clearly
    If my eyesight failed, and I could no more see

For ray

You died in August
                In Winter.
That was fitting.
To die in the dead season.
                        What then?
Did we put you in the cold ground to rot -
                            to disintegrate?

Can a spirit just cease to exist forever?
I did not know the answer.
I mourned your loss.
Would I really never see your again?
Were you now nothingness -
                      you who was once so vital?

Spring came, and Autumn and Summer, with Winter again -
And I still grieved.
But now I was absorbed again in life,
                It did go on.
The garden grew, it needed my attention.
                          Spring came again
and this time I was aware of it -
of the dead wood quickening with life.
Tiny green shoots appearing, growing -
                          bursting forth into flower
to gladden our hearts with their colour and perfume.
The lilac tree which a few short weeks ago seemed
to be a bundle of dead sticks
Was now vibrant and blossoming.

You died.
                You were dead.

Are you dead still?
Is a plant a tree, a shrub
                worth more than a man?
You too must surely be alive once more
in some realm unseen, unknown to us,
Your spirit must surely have lived on
                              for it was beautiful -
more beautiful than any plant.
Is spring telling us of hope and resurrection?
                I pray that it be so.

a Loving Touch

You smile as you pass me the sugar
Touch my arm as you pass by my chair
Take my hand when we walk out together
And show the whole world that you care.

A look and a smile can speak volumes,
A touch is comfort indeed
To have you beside me as we go through life
Is all I will ever need.

HOW?

Love came into my life
And the world glowed bright
Love went away
And it was endless night.

Now you are gone
And joy has taken flight.
The world is grey
I cannot see the light.

I reach out my hand
But you're not there.
I look - and all I see
Is your empty chair.

Your smile, your warmth, your touch.
All gone from me now.
I know I must go on
Please tell me how?

DESTINY

Limitless horizons stretched before you -
life held no boundaries then.
The world was yours for the taking.
You rushed to meet it- savoured it
drank it offerings to the full
you gloried in it.
The good and the bad came in their turn
you accepted them as your due.
And turned them to your advantage.
Oh yes! Life was sweet
Bountiful were her gifts.
Adversity, you met with head held high
daring it to overcome your spirit
all the days of your life you revelled in living.

And now you battle death.
With pride and dignity, you hold it at bay
daring it to overcome you.
Your unquenchable spirit rises
to this last challenge
as you face the inevitable.
With one last valiant gesture
you acknowledge its existence -
allow it into your mind,
and bid it welcome.
Then prepare to launch yourself
into death's dark journey
eagerly anticipating the unravelling
of life's remaining mysteries.

Limitless horizons stretch once more before you -

Times Past

Remembrance of times past still lingers in my heart.
Your face - a little blurred at the edges now -
memory aided by photos - what if there were none?
Often had my fingers traced the line of your cheek
felt the smooth curve of your lips.
'Why?' you asked. I did not answer.
I had thought 'What if I should go blind
would I then remember your face?'
But it was not to be blindness that needed
the memory of your well-loved features.
You went away. Forever.
Can my fingers yet see
the contours they so lovingly followed?
Sometimes for a fleeting second it is all there
just as it used to be.
But mostly it has faded
like colours left too long in sunlight.
Only shadows flit
where once your energy filled the space.

But now I no longer need your defined appearance.
You are there when I call on you
with a feeling of warmth - a feeling of sadness -
and love.
The remembered warmth of our love is always there.
It eases just a little the ache of loneliness
And helps me to bear the emptiness you left behind
With a memory of times past.

LOVE LOST

I walk alone, where once we walked together.
Grey skies and leafless trees reflect the emptiness I feel.
The sun comes up – the sun goes down
The earth spins timelessly on its way.
I grow a little older with each passing year -
A little more alone.
The hollow in my heart remains.
Life and laughter still go on.
But what are life and laughter without love?
Empty echoes resounding down the halls of time.
How can I forget the warmth, the closeness of love?
The joy of sharing, the togetherness?
Little remembered acts of kindness
That spoke of caring.
These things are not forgotten -
As you are not forgotten – nor ever will be
Though you are gone these many years.

Through the softness of moonlight
The clarity of the light of day
I walk alone.
And remember the feel of your hand in mind
As once we had walked together.

I THINK OF YOU

When I think of your
I think of light -
Light, lighting up the darkest corners of my heart.
Your words glow in the ashes
of the fires of my imaginings.
They weave patterns
like sunlight chasing shadows.
I feel the sun grow warm
beneath my skin.
Always I hear your voice
from deep within an ocean of silence
like water dancing in my hands.
When I listen to your words
I can smell the scent of jasmine
see the light sing on the wings of swallows
hear the ripple of water over stone
and feel a sense of peace -
Peace - deeper than dreams -
So deep, it is all there is in the whole wide world.

To a Friend

May your days be filled with sunshine
    and your nights with dreamless sleep
May you walk forever with loyal friends
    and never have cause to weep

Come with me to the mountains
    where the air is pure and clear
And the bellbirds' song is wafted along
    the treetops far and near

Let us sit by the side of a running creek
    in silence - our hearts in tune -
As we drink in the sun and the wind and the sight
    of the beautiful gums in bloom

In the mist and the rain may the beauty remain
    of the everlasting hills
As we walk side by side in joy and in pain
    while with hope our hearts are filled

For you are my friend, and I love you dear
    to my troubled heart you bring peace
With you beside me I have no fear
    your presence brings sweet release

So stay by my side, dear friend of mine
    and hold my hand tight in yours
Let me borrow your strength when my courage fails
    lift me up like a bird that soars

Over the hilltops and over the sea
    and way beyond the blue
Let my spirit soar free above the earth
    because of a friend like you

CHILDHOOD

Dandelions and daisy chains,
    Butterflies and bees
Children laughing joyfully,
    Running as they please.

Chase the gulls that circle,
    Over sparkling sand
Catch the white sea-ohorses
    That vanish in your hand.

Flying kites that hover
    High up in the blue
Sailing through the fluffy clouds
    Waving back to you.

Swimming in the river
    Fishing from a log
Paddling an old canoe
    Playing with the dog.

The wonderful world of childhood,
    The way it used to be,
When all the world was young and gay
    And pleasures were for free.

Ninja Mutant Turtles,
    Nintendo and Star Wars,
Commodore Computers,
    Zapping men from Mars.

Nightmare and Hatari,
    Donkey Kong, Hang On,
Batman and Megadrive,
    And so it goes on.

The world is growing older
    And childhood pleasures change
With each new generation
    There comes a brand-new range.

Today they seem more violent
    Than they ever were before,
With sophisticated weapons
    More deadly than of yore.

Instead of playing rounders
    With friends upon the green,
The kids today seem happier,
    Just staring at a screen.

And shooting anything that moves,
    Then toting up the score
They don't need mates to play with -
    No – not anymore.

They would not want my pity,
    I can't help it, just the same
I feel there's something missing,
    When just one can play a game.

Last Sunday I was at the beach
    With some little friends of mine,
We took along a bat and ball -
    The weather, it was fine.

We tossed the ball and ran and laughed,
    The world was full of glee
I'm glad not everything has changed
    From the way it used to be.

To Dream Dreams

You touched my heart as no-one ever did,
The beauty of your soul shines
Through in everything you do
Your clarity of vision, like a child's
Direct and true,
Sees the wonders of the world
And hears its music, soft and new.

The simplicity of thought and words
You share in verse with others.
You give of yourself without reserve
In the songs you sing for lovers.

You make me dream dreams – fantasise,
Of mountains, misty in the light
Of fairies at the bottom of the garden,
And lullabies that sing through the night.

You give me a talisman to hold on to
When darkness falls and I can see no light.
The comfort of your words is with me,
When the stars are no longer shining bright.

In my heart there is a pain of yearning -
A longing for what can never be.
Why must these desires return to haunt me,
Just when I thought my heart was Oh! so free?

Harmony

My thoughts return ever to the mountains.
I find peace there in high places.
My mind is swept clean by the wind
As it cries out in a thousand voices.
My thoughts rise ever upwards
Like an eagle in flight
As it soars ever nearer to the heavens.
There I can rest in harmony with nature -
Perhaps because it also seems
A little nearer to God.

My Friend James

Streetwise, cheeky, his life is full of zest
My young friend, Jamie, can be an awful pest!
    How about a game of cards, let's go for a walk,
    Read me some poetry he sure knows how to talk.

Let's go down to the lake and maybe fly a kite
Let's stick our feet in the water and hope the fish don't bite.
    Let's climb up the poppet head it's got an excellent view.
    You climb up the poppet head and I'll look at you.

Watch me climb the ladders, and then swing to and frow
Watch me on the slippery-slide, see how fast I go.
    Don't walk UP the slippery-slide - that's not what it's about.
    I know, but it is much more fun! And he's off with a shout.

What's to eat? I'm hungry. So what else is new?
I suppose you want a hot dog? OK that will do.
    I'll pick you some nice wattle as we walk along the track.
    Thanks - but that's illegal - and you can't put it back.

Can we read some poetry? Yes – you can read to me.
OK. I'll get the book down, and then we'll have to see
    Which one will I read first? Maybe 'The Mooch of Life'.
    You'd better read it properly, or you will be in strife.

There's never a dull moment with my youthful friend around.
He talks non-stop, and all the day, with energy abounds.
    He keeps me young and busy, and if truth be told,
    When he spends the weekend with me, then I am twelve years old.

Thirteen

It's your birthday tomorrow,
What would you like?
A football, a skateboard, or maybe a bike?
But no, these things you do not need.
I have something to give you
That I hope will please.

I'll give you my time
When you want to talk.
I'll listen to you
We'll go for a walk.
I'll encourage you in your latest quest.
Whatever it is, to do your best.
I'll read you some poetry to nourish your soul
And I'll help you try to reach your goal.
I'll each you to share and to think about others,
To always play fair and not cheat your brothers.
And when you don't listen, and behave like a brat,
I'll punish you to teach you, you just can't do that.
I'll teach you to stand up for yourself when it counts
And not be too influenced by other accounts.
I'll praise you when you do something unselfish and free,
And I'll love you, because you matter to me.

The Drover
For my brother Alan

My brother, he's a drover,
And he's getting on a bit.
He's been at it since he was a lad,
And he was fighting fit.

Things are different now out on the track,
From what they were back then,
There are motor bikes and fridges,
And the cattle are in a pen.

But some things never change much
There's your horses and your dogs,
And a roaring fire to camp beside.
And you still having plenty of logs.

And your tucker, it is much the same
But cooked on a BBQ,
For bread you still make damper,
And chuck everything in a stew.

You ride your motorbike up front
To check what lies ahead.
For feed and water can still be scarce -
Without them your cattle are dead.

But it's still a long and dusty day
In the saddle behind the mob.
To keep them moving on their way,
With the help of your trusty dogs.

And the nights are just as peaceful
As you camp beneath the moon,
And share a yarn around the fire.
But sleep comes all too soon.

He's getting too old to be on the track.
To be following the watercourse
But it's in his blood, and he'll never stop
While he can mount a horse.

I fancy they'll find him one of these days
By his camp-fire – now gone cold.
Sleeping his last sleep with his horse and his dogs
'Neath the stars he loved of old.

remember?
For Alexandra

You looked so French, so chic, sitting opposite me,
Sucking the froth from your cappuccino.
A beret so jauntily on your short, soft curls
You fitted in so well with the whole atmosphere of The Cross.
I could only drink chocolate -
That made me feel an outsider.
Our drinks finished, we wandered further afield.
Sydney was new to me, and you were my guide
I loved it all - Hyde Park, the Museum, the Harbour, the ferry -
It was all somehow foreign to me - exciting and new.

Our next stop was - what else? - A book shop
We could both lose ourselves there for an hour.
Our mutual love of books, poetry, plays,
The written word in all its shapes and forms -
That was our bond – the basis of our friendship.
An hour later we emerged triumphant without spoils to share.
And then fell about laughing.
A chance in thousands -
Among our treasures we saved till last
The one book that was our special find -
The smallest and lowliest in the shop,
And yes, you guessed it -
It was the same book - Gitanjali!

Twenty years on, the empathy is still there.
I read the poems you sent me, and there it was,
My favourite of all quotations
But you had incorporated it in your poetry - not I.
'Vanity of vanities. All is vanity saith the Lord'.

Though never out of words, I see you rarely these days,
But friendship endures.
Much water has flowed under the bridge since those carefree days
Even though our paths have led in different directions
The fine thread of friendship still connects us to each other.
Together with the shared memories we hold in common.

Greetings from across the sea
For Royale

Bright eyed and outgoing
Confident and free,
You rush forward to meet me
After your journey across the sea.
Tough you have never met me
You know that I love you.
Your parents have shown you photos
And you're willing to love me too.

Six years old, and bright as a button,
You have no fears, no qualm
You have tried all the things a little girl can,
And not come to any harm.
You have no fear of the water
You swim like a fish and dive
You roller-skate and you snow-ski,
And a horse you've learned to ride.
You graduated from kindergarten
With a cap and gown and all.
You're a big girl now
Or so you've been told.
You don't cry when you fall.

You are a child of the nineties
A product of the U S of A
You love your visit to Australia,
With your Aussie cousins you play.
Your Dad takes you to his old school
To meet the teachers now -
You sit in on a class or two
And show the other kids how.
You learn some Aussie songs and rhymes,

And teach us some of yours.
You give a concert to entertain
And sing without a pause.
You play football with your Daddy,
And we all join in with glee.
And then you say, 'please read to me',
And climb upon my knee.

I must leave first to go back home
You come to the bus with me
And hold my hand as they close the doors
That separate you from me.
You call out to me "I love you',
As the bus then pulls away
I cry for miles, and will never forget
Your shining face that day.

I send you letters from time to time
Now that you're back home again.
But it's not the same, and I miss you so
When will I see you again?

I've promised one day before you're too old
I will fly across the sea
To Los Angeles where you live and grow
I hope you'll remember me.

Have no regrets

Pink, fluffy fairy-floss lines the streets -
It must be spring already!
But no! The seasons are confused,
Though the blossoms are so heady.

I love it when the buds appear
On all the leafless branches,
And clouds and clouds of beauty form,
and the bleak, grey world enhances.

I know that winter soon must pass
And give way to pleasanter weather.
My heart rejoices at the glories to come
My spirits are light as a feather.

Each year, as each fresh season passes
A tinge of sadness fills me,
To die is not so terrible.
But oh! To miss all that beauty.

A lifetime does not seem long enough
To savour the beauties around us
To smell the sweet scent of blossoms galore,
As spring comes along without fuss.

When that day comes when we realise
That the seasons left are rationed,
Let us appreciate all the more
The beauty with which they're fashioned.

Spring with its flowers and blustery days
Summer so green and gold
Autumn with bright leaves colouring the world
And winter so starkly cold.

Let us cherish each season while we can
So precious is every day.
And have no regrets that we missed it all,
When we too shall pass away.

The Carousel

High-stepping horses, prancing along,
Round and around to the lilt of a song
Children laugh gaily,
As faster it goes
Riding their steeds,
With their heels and their toes.
How I'd love just to mount one
And ride far away,
Over the hill-tops, and across the bay,
Till the land disappeared
And over the sea
We'd ride on forever,
My charger and me.

My Song of Joy

It is a glorious Spring Day!
An overwhelming feeling of love for the world
and everything in it
surges through my being.

I am alive! I can see and hear and smell the blossoms.
I am part of all the beauty around me
It sings inside my head
of joy and love and laughter
I am richly blessed.

I have friends who shower me with kindness,
and love
far beyond my deserving.
They hold me safe in a cocoon of caring.

My spirits dances in the sunshine
Up to the clouds and beyond.
I rest upon the wind and
gently drift on warm currents of air
down to the green earth below.

I am filled with happiness
I am filled with gratitude.

To be alive - to be loved -
on a sunny Spring Day,
with soft breezes wafting a scent of flowers
along the sparkling air

This must surely be a foretaste of paradise.
I can only be grateful
and give thanks for the wonders of the world
and the wonderful people in it.

Vale Hal

No more shall we hear you comfort
The lonely and the lost.
You helped so many who were down and out,
And did not count the cost.

You listened - something rare today
You listened and sympathised
You passed no moral judgements
You never criticised.

Just held out a friendly helping hand
To those who's need was greatest
You went to bat for the underdog.
For him you demanded justice.

I was among the lonely ones
Who listened, but never rang
When my darling died, as you did
And left me with many a pang.

Your words of comfort to others -
I took them for my own.
I did not need to talk to you
Though you were close as the telephone.

Your friends from the airways are legion.
They are loyal and staunch and true.
And even though you may never have met
They valued a friend like you.

We'll all miss you, Hal, you were one of a kind,
A rare and special man,
And wherever you are you'll be selling your wares
As only Toddy can.

The Rainbow

I saw a rainbow the other day.
Out of an inky sky it appeared,
and coloured the world.

My life has been inky of late filled with clouds
of dark foreboding.
Worry settled like a black cloud on my brow.
a stone became a fixture in my stomach.
I was ever aware of the sword of Damocles
hanging by a thread over my head.

I awoke from a sweet, dreamless sleep, refreshed -
and remembered.
Fear became my constant companion.
It froze my brain.

I tried to think of all the old cliches -
Lights at the end of tunnels,
darkness before the dawn,
clouds have silver linings -
But somehow, I was not impressed
I know they are truisms,
but I am too far gone in fear for them to console me.

Then I saw a rainbow the other day.
The sheer beauty of its delicate colours
Against a background of darkness
struck a chord in my being.
It unfroze my brain for long enough
To allow a fragment of hope to enter.
Now I am buoyed up by the sight of that rainbow
which bought a measure of peace
to my heart
and enchanted me with its beauty.

The Spirit of Delight

The gold is on the wattle and the sky is almost grey
The tree outside my window arbours parrots, bright and gay
    Alighting on the branches bare, they are a glorious sight.
    Their brightness lightens up my day, and fills me with delight.

The water in the creek bed rushes rapidly along
With all the rain the creek is full, and sings a merry song,
    As it bounces over rocks and logs and takes all in its way
    Its song delights my senses and brightens up my day.

We take the children to the park where they can run and play
We watch them on the carousel as it circles on its way
    We give them bread to feed the ducks and hear them laugh in glee.
    The laughter of innocent children is sheer delight to me.

There are so many simple things that we see day by day,
That bring joy to our seeking hearts and cheer us on our way.
    They do not cost a fortune, they've been given us for free
    The spirit of delight is there, if we'll only look and see.

Perchance to Dream

I dream alone,
For who would share my dream?
My spirit calls to a kindred spirit,
But who will answer?
I walk wistfully through life
Wondering if I shall ever meet
The voice I hear in my heart.
Is it an illusion?
Did I dream it into existence?
It follows me hauntingly awake and asleep
Accompanied always by a fatalistic sense
of the unattainable.
I dream alone.
Is it not better thus
Than never to dream at all?

Northern Beauty

Bougainvillea in blossom,
    And hot summer nights
Stars you can reach up and touch
    Glistening, sparkling lights,

Jacarandas blooming proudly
    Mauves so soft and warm
Carpets of wondrous beauty
    Underneath their arms.

Creamy, luscious frangipani,
    Heavy-scented in the night
Tropic beauty all around
    Clear, sparkling light.

Poinsettias rich with colour,
    Stark red against white walls.
Flooding all around with brightness
    As twilight falls.

Sometimes I get homesick
    For northern beauties rare
The heat of languid summer days
    And wish I were back there.

Where the sky is always clear and blue,
    And it's never cold and damp.
The sun shines brightly every day
    Like an ever-glowing lamp.

Peace on Earth

We kneel before the manger
On this holiest of nights
And sing of peace - goodwill to men
While the candles flicker bright.

But will it ever happen -
This prayer we pray each year?
How long before the world's convinced
That love is stronger than fear?

That fighting's not the answer
It won't solve our countries woes
That killing people doesn't help,
Even though they are your foes.

Where are the Wise Men of our world,
What gifts have they to bring,
To help restore some sanity
In this sorry scheme of things?

Where nations fight each other
For power and greed and oil,
When all the people really want
Is food for honest toil.

It would be wonderful to think
That peace could reign at last
And nations put away their arms -
That the fighting now is past.

And we would together gather
Around the crib in love,
With the shepherds and the oxen,
And praise the Lord above.

Round the Crib

Around the crib where Christ was born,
Where the oxen and the sheep,
All gathered to pay homage -
A loving watch to keep.

For the Babe was born in a stable
It was the best that they could do
Now I'm sure that in that stable
Lived other creatures too.

Like rats and mice, for instance,
Playing around in the straw
And where rats and mice are present
There's a pussycat for sure.

So I like to think that a pussy cat
Was present at Christ's birth,
And knelt with the other animals
While choir sang 'Peace on Earth'.

THE DIGNITY OF LABOUR

The festive seasons rolls round once more,
But not so festive for the thousands of the poor
    People whose jobs have been taken away
      They must now feed their families without any pay.

They join the long queues to collect the dole,
With bitterness eating into their soul.
    They don' want handouts, they just want a job,
    To work for their living – be one of the mob.

But now they must accept their fate,
And take what they can get from the State.
    Can it give them back their dignity and pride
    When their days are spent with work denied?

You politicians in your ivory towers,
We, the people gave you your powers
    So please do something to ease the plight
    Of the jobless poor - hey have the right

To hold you responsible for their sorrow.
All they want is a better tomorrow
    If you can't promise that, then you shouldn't be there,
    Or is it a case of - 'you just don't care'?

The Dying Year

The year is dying amid the winds of change
The old order goes - where will the new one range?
What changes have been wrought to be tired old world,
As history a brand-new flag unfurled?

A year that started with war and greed
Gas masks and 'smart weapons' and victims who bleed
Oil-fires and oil-spills and cormorants who died,
That man might keep the riches that oil implied.

A war that ended with one hundred thousand dead
And night turned into day while oil-fires fed.
In other countries other men took up arms against their brothers,
In conflicts that are raging still - while peace returned to others.

And hostages came home at last,
Their long imprisonment now past,
And sadness turned at last to joy,
As freedom's gains they could employ.

And the birds still sing in the branches,
And flowers still bloom in the Spring
No matter what the world does
Or the changes that it brings.

And there were acts of heroism
All across the nation,
As flood and fire and famine raged -
For some there was salvation,
As courage helped to save their lives,
They were an inspiration,

As the old year fades away to the ringing of the bells,
And the old order changes as we see the death-knells
Of things we thought would never change -
but change it seems they will
We pray God it's for the better
that hope is living still.

THE VISIT
For Hugh

With a smile that is warm and friendly
You come to my door.
Energy radiates from you, like a dazzling sun,
'And how's yourself?' you ask,
In your own inimitable Irish way.
'And how's the boy?'
'Come in.'
A quick visit.
Smiles and laughs and jokes.
A chat that is full of tenderness and care.
Concern on your face as you leave,
A quick squeeze of the arm for reassurance
And you are on your way.
To visit yet one more of the sick and lonely
To give a little more of your cheerfulness and energy.
You bring comfort and joy –
for a few minutes each day when you call
You lighten for just a little while
Hearts burdened with sorrow
And we can never thank you enough
For the love and care so generously given
From a heart as big as the whole wide world.

Life: a Celebration

A man has died that we might live
He gave us a second chance
When He arose from out the grave
Our lives He did enhance.
Let us celebrate life and live it to the full.
It is here, it is now, today.

Let us live each moment and drink to the brim
Of its laughter and tears and
whatever it brings,
No matter how short our stay.
We get no more chances
So use the ones we have
Don't sit and watch them fade away.

GOOD FRIDAY

And what do we celebrate today?
A death.
Yes, a death.
For after this day death shall no more
have dominion over us.
This death has killed death forever
And from its ashes rises hope and life.
Forever more will they replace death.
This death has freed us from extinction
And given us the light of two thousand years -
The light that shines in the darkness
To be our guide for all eternity.

NIGHT SONG

I lie in the darkness and listen.
Endless seconds tick away.
Thousands of them filling the night
As slowly and inexorably they march on.

Outside my window the air vibrates
With the haunting perfection of a magpie's song.
Why are you're not asleep, bright bird?
For whom are you singing your wistful song?
I look out into the dark night but cannot see you
Your song trills timelessly on
As the slow seconds tick the night away.

Soon the before-dawn light
Makes shadows in the garden.
Trees and shrubs assume their daytime shapes.
But the ageless splendour of your lilting song goes on.

I am glad of your company, bright bird.
Would that I could raise my voice as you do
And send my lonely cry
Echoing through the still night.
Would that someone would answer.

a friend

The comfort of knowing that you are there
In the deep, hidden recesses of my mind
Tucked away like some happy secret
I would share with no-one.
I do not need you to be ever-present,
To feature in my daily comings and goings,
In the small and large events of my every-day life.
Yet to know that you, my friend, are there.
What a wealth of difference it makes
How it colours my sometimes colourless world.

The Harvest

The leaves have fallen,
The harvest has been reaped.
The fruits of our labour have been gathered in.
We would give thanks for a season of fruitfulness
A season where love has flourished
In the warmth of the sun,
Nurtured by understanding and tolerance.
A season of striving against all odds
With strength of will and mind to overcome.
We have battled the odds and stood firm.
Now the harvest is ours.
For this we are grateful,
And give thanks.

Daughter of Chernobyl

Weep for your child Oh Mother of Chernobyl.
Weep for the childhood she will never have.
Where are her lovely, long tresses now?
Torn from her head by the bitter wind that blew
and dropped its deadly cargo
Into the lives of innocent children.
Victims of horrific diseases – their lives now a misery -
Weary and sick, worn and hungry,
They have no will - no strength to play
'If only I could feed her', a mother cries,
'If only she could spend some time in clean air'.
Dear God, is it too much to ask -
Food - and clean air? If only -

Pale faces, hairless heads, accusing eyes -
Who did this to them?
They neither know, nor do they care.
Their lives are running out
In weakness and pain and hunger.
But we know.
Now the whole world knows.
How can we ensure it will never happen again?
That it must not happen again?

The world weeps for you.
Oh, Mother of Chernobyl.
For you, and for your children.

a coat of many colours

I wove you a coat of many colours,
Tiny pieces of blue from the sky and sea.
 Green from the trees – so shiny and light,
Russets of Autumn – rich war, and bright.
Reds for the fruits of the earth, I wove,
Gifts of the seasons – ripe in the sun.
A butterfly caught in a glistening web,
Fluttering forever, a glorious sight,
Her wings myriad – coloured pieces of light.

I wove it with threads of gossamer fine,
Entwined with love, and embroidered so fair.
The glory of a rainbow for hope, you will find,
And my heart in the middle please handle with care.
May the love that is woven with these colours so bright,
Bring joy to your heart, and warmth to your sight.

a bunch of flowers

A bunch of flowers, fresh and bright
Sweet smelling in the morning light
Cheering my heart with their colours gay
Spreading their happiness along the way

Tomorrow they will be wilted and worn
Their colours faded, their petals torn
A few more days, they are rank and vile -
Their life is short - such a little while

    So gather ye rose buds while you may
    Sweet flowers bloom for but a day

a Dead Dream

Today I buried a dead dream.
The life had long gone out of it.
Only I did not want to know it.
At the edge of my life I looked on
and endured the silence -
Silence which clamoured so noisily
around me.
Like a butterfly whose life was flickering away.
My dream died.
Dreams, like life, need sustenance.
Before the leaves turned to gold
I buried it in a field of flowers.
It deserved that much.
So be it.

LONG AGO

Oh! There's a voice inside my head,
    that comes from long ago.
From a time when life was simpler,
    and not so full of woe.

It reminds me of those carefree days,
    I spent down on the farm.
With my happy, country cousins
    in a world so full of charm.

We'd eat watermelons off the vine,
    and oh! They tasted great.
With pink juice running everywhere.
    A sticky mess to make.

We would wander through the graveyard
    and read the stories there
Engraved on tombstones oh! so old
    and maybe say a prayer.

We would swing so high in 'Tarzan' vines,
    and roam the bush so free
And then bring the cows home,
    to milk, before our tea.'

And tea was full of goodies
    fresh bread, corn meat and jam,
and golden pats of butter
    and thick, pink slices of ham.

and cream, so thick and yellow,
    to eat with fresh, stewed fruit.
No-one was on a diet then,
    Oh yum! It tasted beaut!

The farm, of course, is no longer there
    the cousins are scattered abroad.
But I'll always remember with love in my heart,
    those golden days I adored.

When Hope Dies

When hope dies, the heart wears out with wanting.
Look at the stark, winter trees
that they should come to this.
Bare, barren bleak and brown.
Where is there hope?
They wait for the sun o wear down the day.
The cluttered heart is swept clean
by the forgiving glow.
It waits to touch and be touched.
We chase after dreams in the diminishing light
of far-off alien stars
But the heart remembers,
when hope dies, love rises like a Phoenix
from the ashes.

when love is born

Out of the depths of loneliness,
from the very fringe of despair,
a voice calls to me to come live again,
join the world in love.
Forget the stony years – full of care
and emptiness.
Feel the earths love beneath your feet,
see the golden light of the moon sailing
across the landscape of your imaginings.
Feel the murmur of the heart
as it sweeps across the stars,
like fireflies flickering in the dusk.
Come, again, let the dead bury the dead.
Come out into the sunlight
where all things sparkle in the richness of light.
Come, live again – for love is the heartbeat of life.

The Quiet Time

summer evenings - the music of cicadas
scent of eucalypts heavy in the air
mellow gold of the fading light
softness, stillness everywhere
birdsong joyous in the glow
of a thousand summers
the tall grass whispers
insects hide in the cracks of trees.
leaves full of golden light
are scattered like rain in the soft breeze
nestled against the tree-trunk
I feel the coarse bark under my hands
living, breathing - I drink it in
a golden glow suffuses the landscape
all things are bright and beautiful
as a solitary bird sings of home
and death and joy and pain
high in the blossoming tree

Perfect Peace

The incredible wonder of perfect peace
Stillness so quiet it is almost deafening.
Mind and heart attuned to each other
And the pervading silence.
The body relaxes, the senses quicken,
At something so unexpected,
Wondering what the joyous sensation might be.
Time and motion are suspended
The mad race to nowhere ceases.
Just halts for a while
And takes time out to pause and reflect.
To marvel at the glory of the world
And all that is in it.

The stars in their heavens look down
At the everlasting foolishness of man,
Forever chasing what he can never have.
And overlooking he wondrous joy
That is there within his grasp
Should he but pause for long enough
To reach out, and take it in his hands.

now

Now is the moment I was born
The moment of 'Now I am here'.
Now is when I awoke this morn
To a new day bright and clear.

Now is the present and the past
Now is this living minute.
Now is all the time we have.
So we can glory in it.

There is no future – it never comes
It's only the present we live in
And all the past 'nows' now are gone.
So seize the time we've been given.

recession

Peeling paint on shop fronts
Rust on iron railings
Tattered fly-specked posters
Empty windows gaping

Recession

No more helpful chemist
No more hot-bread shop
No more friendly butcher
Just gaps along the block.

Recession

Our little local village,
Once so bright and gay
With friendly neighbours chatting
As they went along their way.

Recession

Now it is depressing
To see those blank eyes stare,
To miss the friends whose livelihood
Is no longer there.

Depression

Dole queues snake across the land,
Blank faces grimly staring,
Jobs are non-existent
Is anybody caring?

Recession

In homes across the nation
Tempers flare and rage
Shortened by anxiety
A symptom of the age.

Depression

Soul-destroying worry
Creeps into the heart.
Is here still no end in sight,
No way to make a start?

Depression

We pray this suffering soon will end,
To save thus stricken band,
Before Despair takes over
And reigns across the land.

Gone

Because I want to hear your voice
No need to murmur low:
Because I want to feel your touch
Soft as moonlight's glow:
Because I want to smell your scent
Like roses blooming near:
Because I want to see your face
That is to me so dear:
Then I will love you from the heart
Wherever you may be:
And I will keep your memory true
Though you are gone from me:
Always in my thoughts you'll be
When the fire is flickering low:
You are my love till the end of time
Till the tide forgets to flow.

wonder

Children laughing
Dogs barking -
Happy sounds are they.
Birds calling
Leaves falling
All across the way.

Alone I sit and ponder
On a world
So full of wonder
Sun shining
Clouds smiling
O'er the wide blue yonder.

Happiness
in small things -
Sights and sounds and smells.
Trees rustling
Bees buzzing
And the joyous peal of bells.

The smell of freshly cut grass
On a warm summer's day
The morning call of birdsong
To greet a brand-new day.

The cool crisp feel of morning dew
On every blooming flower
The cleansing rain that falls to earth
In a lightning summer shower.

I talk to the birds
I talk to the trees.
I hold the rough trunk in my arms.
I lay my cheek on the tangy bark,
And succumb to all their charms.

Oh! How I love the little things
That greet me every day.
I pray that life may never take,
That feeling of wonder away.

The Seasons Change

There is a sadness deep inside me
Another season gone.
Change all around me I see.
The highs and lows of summer past
are spent, never to be recaptured.
Please wait! Don't go!
This summer I was almost happy
Just let me hold it for a while -
Just look at it and remember.
Time moves too fast for me now
I would cherish the golden days
And the nights at warmed my heart.

I would give thanks for a season of gladness -
A season of love and beauty,
Which may never come again

WaITInG

The old lady lay in her narrow bed.
My cat made a bigger bump in her bedclothes than she did.
She was just skin and bone now, shrunken with age,
And the stroke that had laid her low.
They took one leg off last year
Gangrene they said, caused by inactivity
Well, what did she care she wasn't using it anyway.
George, she called the stump
'Knit me a sock for George, he gets cold', she said,
Some of the nurses were all right,
But one of them pinched her chocolates,
Always the best ones too.
The same one always hurt her when she was dressing her.
Hurt her little arm, she said.
That was the one that had shrunk
And stayed pressed across her stomach.
They would take her out on the verandah soon
She could watch the frilly lizard from there.
He lived in the bush next-door

It would soon be morning-teatime.
She looked forward to that.
The food was good, but hard to eat without teeth.
And hers didn't fit any more.
It was Monday. Her daughter would be here soon
She looked forward to Mondays.
Maybe she would bring her a sliced mango.
That was her favourite. Easy to eat, too.
But it was a long wait between Mondays.
Five years of the same routine, the same people.
How many more years before she would be allowed to go?
She wasn't bitter. God would look after her.
But she really was so tired of it all.

early memories

The sound of a cross-cut saw, I remember,
    Far back in my childhood when I was very young
The sad, brown eyes of the cows I loved,
    Patience personified and the songs we sung.

My father cracking a raw-hide whip -
    He had plaited it himself – I can still hear the crack
Though it was a very long time ago
    The sound that it made still takes me back.

Riding on a sled with the cream-can
    One horsepower it was then
To deliver the cream to the pick-up point,
    And then riding home again.

I remember an old lady we visited.
    A second cousin once removed I think
She was the oldest person I had ever seen,
    But she made me a wonderfully, tasty drink.

It was made from fresh berries she'd picked herself
    And crushed with lemons and limes.
I can taste it yet though it's many a long year
    Since this old, old lady died.

And I can smell the heat and taste the dust
    As I climbed upon the fence
And sat and watched the sun set,
    And dreamed of a journey hence.

But even in my childhood dreams
    How could I ever imagine
The world as it would turn out to be
    The kind of world I'd live in...

As I look back on those early years,
    For the old days I don't pine.
Just a few random glimpses of how things were
    But I cherish them – they're mine.

Today

Death will come when life is over -
and life is a fragile thing.
A tapestry we weave with deeds -
with acts of kindness
and with words
we never meant to say.
The things we meant to do, but didn't,
the words of love we never said.
The thanks we forgot to mention,
the starving people left unfed.
They are a part of the broad pattern
our lives are forming day by day.
When we look back will we be happy
at what we see
or will we say -
I did not mean it to be like this -
how could I have gone so far astray?

THE LAND THAT TIME FORGOT

Down where the Murray flows,
And river gums grow tall
Where parrots fly beyond the sky
You can hear the mopoke call.

It's a land of stark, clean beauty
A land that's got the lot
Blue skies, fresh air – it has more than its share
It's the land that time forgot.

To sit on the sandy beaches
To gaze far out to the plains
To follow the mighty water course
As it twists and turns in vain.

Over the roots of mighty trees
Long lost in the rivers flow
It winds its way by night and day
Where the gusty breezes blow.

It's a land of fertile pastures
A land where crops grow lush
A land where sheep and cattle graze
A land of untamed bush.

A land I love with a love that's free.
A land that's in my blood.
A land that haunts me in my dreams -
The land of the Murray mud.

I must come back to her mighty shores
To feel the power she's got.
This land I love with all my heart.
The land that time forgot.

Thank You

From the long dead past your face rises up before me.
Clearly I see it now -I hear the music and see the dancers
and smell the Californian Poppy.
Obligatory it was then.
And my partners so young - as I was.
But the face I see is not in the midst of all that gaiety
it is in another room - a small grotty room -
a seat along one wall - the Ladies Room.
There you sat, not really caring what went on around you
just knitting quietly.
The whole long evening you sat there
while we danced the night away.
Oh, the selfishness of youth - the desperation -
the need to be like all the others.
And you gave it to me.
I was not permitted out alone, so you came.
Could I ever really thank you for that gift of youth?
But for you it would have passed me by.

The Worst of Times

They cut down the forests
Denuded the soil
Killed off the animals
Lived without toil

With spray-cans and plastics
They polluted the earth
Without giving thought
To what they were worth

The sky is the limit
Yes, once that was true
But now there's a hole there
Way up in the blue

The earth's getting warmer
Than it ought to be
And as each year passes
In comes more of the sea
It eats away more
Of our seashore so grand
So now we have water
Where once there was land

Our soil is eroded
Blown away by the gales
With no shelter to stop them
Our crops, they will fail

With more hungry mouths
Than our earth can support
No wonder there's famine
And diseases are caught

They spread through the country
The kill far and wide
They cannot be halted
Though science has tried

I fear for this planet
Once so bountiful and free
In fifty years' time I wonder
How will it be?

THE BEST OF TIMES

It was the very best of times
The world was young and free
And forests were still forests
Fish still swam in the sea

Our lakes were not polluted
There was no hole in the sky
Our planet was not dying
There was no need to cry

There were no threatened species
Our birds flew happily
Our animals in the forest
Never doubted they were free

They did not need protection
For they were left alone
To go forth and multiply
The forest was their own

Yes, it was the very best of times
We all lived side by side
Each gave the other due respect
Trust did in us abide

The Sun Goes Down

The sun goes down
On fields of gentle flowers it lingers
Amid the calm beauty of the landscape.
A pearly glow colours the air
And birds fly home to rest.

I would rest too.
My sun has started its slow descent
Through the mist I see a path
But know not where it leads,
Nor how long the path may be.

The hot sun of my life has burnt itself out.
Winters are getting colder.
The world is getting older.
And I would sit by my fireside
Warm and at rest before the glowing embers.

The Dancing Air

The air is dancing, dancing
The day is blue and gold
The sun is playing peek-a-boo
With life as it unfolds

The air is dancing, dancing
As the leaves fall one by one
They flutter slowly to the earth
They shimmer in the sun

The air is dancing, dancing
A merry jig for all.
Her clothes are bathed in colours bright -
The colours of the fall

The air is dancing, dancing
And I must join the spree
Of dancing air and dancing light
Come! Join the dance with me!

Whispers on the Wind

It comes to be in whispers
Drifting down the ranges tall -
Floating above the city
I can hear its haunting call.

Its calling from the sunny north,
From the land where I was born -
Come back where the sun is shining
Where the air is soft and warm.

Come back to the land that bore you -
To the land of the singing sand
Where jacarandas grow and rivers flow
From mountains to the strand.

Come back to the winter sunshine
To palm trees and wattles gold
To the land of my carefree childhood -
To the land that I loved of old.

'Neath the steely skies of the sodden south
I hear that mystic call
And fair would go where the raintree grow
And blue skies never pall.

I Like Trains

I have seen the bush by moonlight from my bunk whereon I lie
I have watched in dreaming reverie the trees go flashing by
I have seen the semi-trailers on the highways close at hand
As those red-eyed monsters hurtle at full speed across the land.

I have wondered as we linger in some sleepy, outback town
Just what there is to linger for, and why we have slowed down.
I hear the rhythm of the wheels, humming their merry song
As my dreams still linger in my head, they carry me along.

Then off into the night we roar as I dream of other trains
Crossing frontiers in the Orient or miles of endless plains.
Or trains that carry soldiers gone to fight another war
In some far-ff land across the sea, that's not worth fighting for.

Or I'm riding on the Blue Train or the Orient Express,
And everyone I meet's a spy dressed up in fancy dress.
I can feel the long-gone presence of mystery and intrigue
The echoes of another age that seem to be in league.

Or the little chug-chug trains that climb green mountains filled with sheep,
With watercourses running by along the hills so steep.
I have seen these restful places when I've been on other trains
In other countries of the world I dream I'm there again.

Soon the mists begin to rise from every waterhole
As dawn creeps slowly in and brings deep peace into my soul
My eyes are drowsy, I must sleep while the train goes roaring on
And I dream of times and places and train rides that are gone.

Winter of Despair

The steely skies reflect my mood
The bitter cold, deserted streets,
Garbage blowing in the wind,
And foetid smells the nostrils greet.

Huddled bodies in the lanes,
Their eyes look out like tortured things.
No warmth is there for such as these
Despair is all the night-time brings.

Their nights are long, their dreams are short
Lost hours faded with the light.
Lost long ago is hope - she failed
To last throughout the sleepless nights.

No warmth, no hope, no smiling face
To greet them when they wake once more.
Their lives are short, their future bleak
Their world the lot of the hopeless poor.

Those faces haunt me when I go
Back to my world of warmth and love.
I wonder as my pity grows,
Is someone watching from above?

The Spring of Hope

'Twas spring, and hope was in the air
    The world seemed fresh and newly green,
Young things were born across the land
    And life took on a lowing sheen.

The worn and weary of the world
    Beset by woes on every side
Took heart and thought 'I'll start again,
    I won't be beaten by the tide.

When dreams begin to fade I'll wake
    And fight for all that I have willed
I'll not allow my thoughts to dwell
    On longings that can't be fulfilled.'

The warm earth stirs in wonderment
    The pale stars fade, the sun grows warm,
And through the ancient mists I see
    Sweet blossoms all the world transform.

The weary of the world look up
    And see below their tired eyes
A patch of blue to comfort them -
    A tiny glimpse of paradise.

a sign of the times

Lights reflecting on rain-washed streets
Cold and damp the night
Slowly he walks under dripping trees
   His foot dragging.
    Weary, weary is the world,
Many miles he has left behind
On his way to nowhere.
Cosy the lights through the drawn curtains
    The warmth attracts like a moth,
    He peers in the window
Glimpsing other lives.
He was like that once.
Once he had a house with a bright fire
   And cheerful noises.
Noises of Love. And companionship.
Laughter and friendliness were there
Once. But now. Now he has nothing.
   And no-one.
Not even a roof over his head
On this most cheerless of nights.

ever after

Dark the night – and black the water -
Dead leaves drift underfoot.
Desolate the landscape
beneath a starless sky.
Alone he walks with only his thoughts for company,
No birds sing in his dead heart.

What do they know of heaven and hell?
Who know nothing of this torture -
This passion, deep and abiding that lasts a thousand lifetimes?
This loss that is his for all eternity?
Dark, blank spaces that nothing can fill
No warm hand to clasp -
No bright eyes to speak so clearly -
Unspoken words that fill the air.
No firm steps beside him -
Just hollow sounds from a hollow man.
Despair looms dark and uninviting -
like the water,
dank, dead, smelling of rotting carcasses.
Was this his life?
Is this his death?
Is this his ever after?

The Grave

It touched my heart when I read the story
Of three paupers buried with no claim to glory.
No friends to stand by their graves and cry
Not even a glance from a passer-by.

Three people from different walks of life
Lie in one grave after years of strife.
No stone to mark who is buried there
No flowers to show there is someone to care.

Just a few soft petals and a few lumps of earth,
Strewn by someone to show the worth
Of human beings who lived and died
Through hardship and loneliness and sometimes cried.

I shed a tear for the friendless three,
And offered a prayer that wherever they be,
In death they may find what in life they did not
Then their unmarked grave will not matter a jot.

Young Love

In the corner they sat -
Two young people -
So young and so defenceless.
His arm was around her shoulders.
She appeared almost uninterested in what he was saying
He gazed at her with his heart in his eyes.
Then he rested his acned face on her shoulder
As if he were coming home.
All the loneliness in the world gazed out of those eyes.
And the longing for someone to love -
Someone to love him.
They sat, uncaring of the river of faces
That ebbed and flowed on their horizon,
Uncaring of anything outside their sixteen-year-old world.

Then the waitress appeared with two plates of food.
They turned to each other and smiled.
Their smiles as bright as sunbreak.
And with gusto, they attacked their pie and chips.

Last Days On Magnetic Island

I wanted to show you Queensland -
my home for so many years.
But I left it too late
You could scarcely walk by then.
Nevertheless we went.
People helped.
We went by taxi to the beach
And you sat in the shade
And we talked
You sat in the sun one day
And your feet swelled up.

Back at the flat, from your bed
We could see out of the large windows.
We played word games
Till the pain became too great.
Then I would give you another pill.
You didn't like taking them,
You wanted to be alert.
You knew that before long
You would sleep permanently.

The glassed-in fish under water fascinated you.
You took endless photo
Hanging on to the rail with one hand
While you worked the camera with the other.
You didn't want my help
You wanted to do something by yourself.

I cooked barramundi for our dinner.
You liked that and ate it all with relish.
I helped you shower – soaping you
while water poured over us both.
Then I dried you down and dressed you -
like a child.

You knew that when we got home
You would never go out again.
So we lingered on – till at last we had to leave.
You loved my sunny north.
Then we came back home for you to die -
In the cold southern winter.

When Twilight Goes

Her companion is the radio -
Other voices - other woes,
to help forget the loneliness
That comes when twilight goes.

Her man is gone, and her children too,
Gone with the winds that blew.
There's just her cat for company -
She never wanted it so.

The autumn of her life was good -
Oh, why did it have to go?
And take away her health and strength,
And leave her feeling low.

Her man is just a memory now,
That fades as water flows
She hugs it for comfort to her breast,
Just like a faded rose.

Her life goes on as it must go
In the half-light that scarcely glows
While she waits with dread for the loneliness
That comes when twilight goes.

GOLD

Who has seen the dried-out sunlight
    Cast its gold across the land?
In ragged splashes emptying its sheen
    On the fresh-washed sand.

There in pools of shadow
    Lie the daffodils so bright,
Nodding wisely in the morning
    As they capture rays of light.

Fields of mustard plant in flower
    Glow as far as eye can see,
Lighting up the blue horizon
    With a golden melody.

Lonely hills forever rising
    Through the golden air,
Calling to each aching heart
    To come and linger there.

Wattle bravely flaunts its blossoms,
    'Neath a lowering sky.
A patch of gold to warm the heart
    Of every passer-by.

The joy of evening birdsong,
    Each note of liquid gold
Is there if you will listen
    As their glory they unfold.

It's a golden world we live in
    If we but look and see
The beauties God created
    Just for you and me.

Winter's End

Winter's end – a time of longed-for joy
Through the hard, unforgiving season
Lasting one and on with scarce a show of warmth,
Bitter days – bleak and unrewarding
Chill the heart, and bring in their train
Desolate thoughts and grim foreboding.
Rain drumming ceaselessly on the roof
Trees tossed in frenzied gusts by icy winds,
Match the inner turmoil.
Problems assume gigantic proportions
And thoughts, grey as the day, eat away at reason.
Till finally without man's intervention -
Right on due – comes Spring
And with it hope
To raise once more our battered spirits.

LOOKING BACK

As I look back now there is so much to remember
Warm lights in dark houses -
So cosy they looked from the outside.
I, who lived in one room, felt like a little girl
with her nose pressed to the lolly-shop window -
The inside forever out of reach.

A prim landlady - 'you can't boil a kettle after nine-
Don't bring your boyfriend in the house -
Come straight home from work.'
The weather was cold – the atmosphere colder.
So we sat on the windowsill of the pub next door
Freezing on the outside
But with a warm glow uniting us.

I remember the steam trains spraying coal dust over everything-
Their mournful cries echoing my own cry.
As if the entire universe was full of cries.
These same cries are still in my dreams
I can still smell the coaldust,
And still see the lonely young girl
Outside – forever looking in.

a land for all seasons

A land of primitive mountains,
Their pinnacles stark to the sky -
A land of smouldering sunsets
That colour with a radiant dye.

A land that is hushed and breathless
With the heat that rises at noon
A land that ends a glorious day
By the light of a great, white moon.

A land of shining white beaches
Whose waves wash into the shore
In a million sunlit ripples
When the long, bright day is o'er.

A land of lakes and sparkling streams
Whose reflections pure and clear,
Double the beauty of the trees surrounding
The mountains far and near.

A land where gulls cry mournfully,
And the wind blows in from the lee
When ships are framed against an opal sky
On a restless, tossing sea.

This is the land of the Long White Cloud
With beauty at every turn.
In mountains and lakes and glaciers -
A land to which I must return.

Wild Horses

In the wide-open spaces
They go through their paces
They prance and they dance with abandon
Fresh from the hills, they still have their wills
And from man they want not a hand on.

So wild and so free,
Such a joy to see
How their heads toss and turn as they snaffle,
And snort and whirl, and attempt to hurl
Their rider from out of the saddle.

And I feel rather sad
As I watch them get mad.
Their fury is something to see
As they buck and they writhe
And lengthen their stride
In a valiant attempt to break free.

Now their wild days are over
They're no longer a rover
Free to traverse the mountains at will.
With manes and tails flying,
they soar without trying
Now they're broken and captive still.

We were once like those horses -
Untrammelled by forces
That would grind our high spirits to dust.
And take from us joy in life
Replace it with anger and strife
Now we live in a world I can't trust.

Brief Encounter

A day so brilliant, after yesterday's rain,
How could I be so lucky again?
    I boarded the boat in a light-hearted way,
    Looking forward immensely to a day on the bay.

The sea was so green, deep green and bright,
As we got under way in a lovely, soft light
    Sea-swallows swooped and dived all around,
    And hills in the distance with glory were crowned.

The skipper announced he way we would go
To see dozens of islands, we would cruise to and fro.
    His voice was attractive – warm soft and clear
    And I thought I would like him – from what I could hear,

Out in the sparkling waters so green
some penguins were spotted – the first we had seen.
    Bravely riding the waves, they looked little and cute,
    and after we passed them the boat gave a toot.

To see the skipper, I went down below
To find out some things that I wanted to know.
    We talked about birds and the sea until noon
    As two people talk, whose minds are in tune.

I lunched on an island, so green and so bright
Surrounded by beaches of clean, shining white.
    Then returned to the launch for the afternoon's run.
    What a wonderful day! I was having such fun.

Down below I went to see the skipper once more
About what this time, I cannot be sure.
    With a smile of welcome, he ushered me in
    And we talked and we laughed 'till the sun grew dim.

The day was a fading, we were reluctant to part,
A wonderful day that had stirred my heart,
    The way nothing had for a long, long time
    And all I could think of was an old, old rhyme.

We were ships that passed in the night, I thought,
A wonderful day that could come to nought
    But a beautiful memory to take away
    Of a glorious cruise, out there on the bay.

cane country

The train pulled slowly out into the dark night -
headed North. North – I thought
to the land of the cane-fields
Cane trains ran there once.
Are they still there, I wondered?
I pictured them, as I remembered them
Toy trains chugging along through the tall cane.
Flat countryside – miles of rolling fields
with nothing but cane
And the river.
Always we were aware of the river
In flood as it so often was, it was ferocious
Cutting us off from everything – isolating us.

Late afternoon, and the cane fires are blazing – burning off
My cousins – young men full of energy and fun -
How they delighted in coming in from the cane fields
blackened with soot and smoke
And rubbing nit all over me, till I was black too!
Then we must go through the Mill.
I watched as they quickly sewed the bags of sugar,
Showing off to their young cousin.
I didn't ever tell them, but I didn't like the Mill.
The sickly smell of molasses was too overpowering for me.
I was always glad to be back out in the fresh air.

I remembered the clothes on the line
Sheets were always a hazard as was everything white.
If the wind was blowing the wrong way
They would be covered with specks of bagasse -
sticky and dirty. Everything took on a speckled look.
And the smell of molasses came on the wind, too

A special sugar town smell.
A lot of things would have changed now, I thought,
But not the smell. It was a part of it all,
Telling you, you were now in cane country.

And, of course, the cane toads – they were everywhere.
Walk out in to the dark at night and you would step on one
with a horrible squelch.
Drive along the streets, and under every streetlight
you would see dozens of them.
You could not dodge them if you wanted to.
As the car drove over them, you could hear it
pop, pop, pop as they burst
Not my favourite sound.
But that was North Queensland.

And I loved it all.
I could feel my heart expand
To meet the great expanse of cane and sky
The wonderful glow of the sunset
Followed by the brighter glow of the cane fires.

My thoughts followed the train, long after it was lost
in the distance.
I could feel the warmth of the northern sun
See the bright blue of the northern sky
And I felt homesick for the heat and the easy friendships
the music and the laughter, and the casual way of life
That was the North.
I sighed for the past that was dead and gone, never to be recaptured
As I turned to go out into the damp, cold night,
Under the grey skies of my southern home.

Southland in Autumn

Rolling green pastures, dotted with grazing sheep,
Lines of poplars glowing in the golden sun
Reflection on lakes of tranquil hue
Rivulets soft and clear to soothe and dream by
The sweet song of a thrush in a roadside bush,
So much quiet beauty – gentle beauty.

Dark foreboding hills, with rocky escarpments
Sliced out by a giant hand
White water rushing over rocks in cataracts
Rainforest smelling damply of the earth
Stretching far up into the sun.
Awesome beauty – unbelievable grandeur,
Nature in all her shapes and moods,
Kissed by warm sunshine,
Washed by misty rain.
A land of ancient beauty
Coloured by the bright leaves of the fall.

new ideas

Gates closing, minds closing
Shutting out the world,
Shutting in one tiny thought,
In narrowness unfurled.

One little thought in its tiny cell,
Without room to expand.
One little thought that cannot grow,
And spread throughout the land.

It needs another for company
One cannot breed alone.
O open the gates, and open the mind
And for narrowness atone.

Open them wide to new ideas,
To differing points of view.
That one little thought may blossom and yield
A thousand ideas anew.

The Old Soldier

No one listens much when he talks
They've heard his tales before
He's told then over and over
In the long years since the war.

They've all forgotten those terrible years -
The ones told enough to remember.
They don't want to listen any more
When he tells of that grim September.

When he talks of the time when he saw his mate die -
A young man as he was then.
His life cut short by the bullets that flew
And hit him, again and again.

In front of his eyes his young life ran out
Screaming in pain and horror
And all he could do was look on and weep,
As he held his hand in sorrow.

With his arms around him, he died in fear
Not quite fully understanding
What had happened to him, and why it should.
He was so young and undemanding.

How could he forget those tragic scenes?
He'd dreamed of them year after year.
Though time did help, the memory was there
It would not just disappear.

So, when Anzac Day comes around each year
With old friends he joins the parade.
They understand, and will listen to him
As he remembers his fallen comrade.

Impermanence

Don't put all your eggs in one basket,
So often I've been told.
But I really do have so few eggs,
And my other baskets are holed.

When I love, I love with all my heart
I'm loyal to friends for life
But they die, and go away and leave me,
To cope alone with trouble and strife.

Or they go far away to the ends of the earth,
Where I can see them no more
And can never again be filled with joy
As I see them come through the door.

My pets grow old and sick, and die
I grieve for them, one by one.
My heart breaks a little as each one goes,
And I fear there is more to come.

Will nothing stay in this shifting world,
For more than a month or two?
Where can I love and not be hurt?
My dreams not smashed in two?

Shall I then love less – will it not hurt so much,
As the next dream shatters and rends?
But without love and care how is it possible
To make and keep new friends?

As the old disappear in this changing world,
It is harder to find the new.
They are so busy living their hectic lives.
Dear God, I just need a few.

Please don't take away everyone I love,
By death or changing lifestyles.
I need someone to accompany me
As I walk the weary miles.

The weary miles that go on to the end
Of our stay in this vale of tears.
Please leave me a voice to encourage and cheer
And soothe my lonely fears.

THE OLD MAN

His hair was white, his fingers gnarled,
    He had that weather-beaten look
He sat on a stool he had brought with him,
    And out of his pocket, he took a book.

We passed him by on our way up the track
    He was in a corner, beneath a tree
We ambled along, looking right and left,
    To try to find what we came to see.

We were looking for a long-dead celebrity
    We knew his grave was somewhere near.
We just wanted to pay homage – a mark of respect.
    But first we must find it – a tall order, I fear.

And so it proved, we walked for miles,
    And many a tombstone verse we read
Till finally we came in triumph, at last,
    To where our hero lay – a stone at his head.

We paid our respects and wandered away,
    Back up the path we had earlier walked.
We passed by the tree where the old man still sat,
    reading aloud from the book he had brought.

It was nursery-rhymes he read – to whom?
    As the tears down his cheeks, they trickled and ran.
He didn't look up as we made our way past
    He was miles away, in a world of his own.

We'll never know what his story was -
    That sad, old man, sitting there all alone.
But I murmured a prayer as we walked on by,
    That God would send comfort to one of his own.

THE DARKEST NIGHT

Ten paces long – six paces wide:
Emptiness – solitude:
the world shut out.
A bolted door – a high window:
Panic:
Silence, like the grave:
Dark, darker than night,
Not a vestige of light.
Where is the sky?
Where are the stars?

The walls close in
Tighter and tighter
Suffocating.
Alone in an alien world.
Where has my world gone?
Where are my people?

Alone in the darkness
I hear nothing – see nothing.
This way lies madness.

The scream inside my head bursts forth
No one answers.
I cry out again
Hear me – talk to me.
Still no answer.
Silence – complete.

Is this the way the world ends?
Is this the way my world ends?
Alone – afraid – deserted?

THE FADED LADY

She was a little, faded lady,
And I watched her sitting there.
While the throng milled all around her
but still she did not stir.

She had been sitting there for ages,
So still, like a little mouse
And I began to wonder if she needed help
To get her back to her house.

When along came a woman and a little girl,
And her eyes lit up so bright
And the smile that shattered that faded face
Came like a burst of light.

I was glad that somebody loved her,
That faded lady sitting there.
As the little girl took her wrinkled hand
And led her off without a care.

Abandoned

'I can't take care of her anymore',
The note on the wheelchair read.
And the old lady sitting in it
Wished that she were dead.

For a long time now she had been shuffled
From one home to another,
The children did not want her
To them she was too much bother.

But what could she do, she was old and tired,
And could no longer cope alone.
If they didn't want her there was no one else.
They were all she could call her own.

And now they had taken her to the hospital
And left her – just dumped her there
Leaving her for someone else to mind
And walking off without a care.

How could they do this to her,
Who had reared them for twenty years
Giving all her love and care and thought
And now it would end in tears.

Surely death was preferable to this agony
Of knowing that no one cared
Of being a burden on a stranger
Instead of joy to those she'd reared.

I DID NOT WANT TO KNOW

She told me of her death.
How it would come soon
And how she was buoyed up
by hope and love
As if God were holding her aloft,
Cradling her in His caring arms
Where no harm could come to her.
She told me of her happiness -
the feeling of contentment and well-being
As if the worst the world could do to her was done
and death – the preferred option.
She told me this with joy in her voice.
I believed her.
But still – I wept.

arms

Only a million, and cheap at that,
Considering what it will do -
Wipe out a city in one fell swoop
Is that grand enough for you?

And here's something even you can afford,
It's tailored for the man in the street
Just press down the button, and let it rip
Look out! Or you'll be dead meat.

Let's make it even more easy to kill,
So we won't have to think what we do.
Just 'ready, aim fire' and away we go
Is that simple enough for you?

But we all want peace – I hear you cry,
Peace and goodwill to all men
Of course we do, and here's how we'll get it,
By pulling the trigger again.

Just make sure it's faster and deadlier
Than the one on the other side
And remember to hit the button first
Then peace will with you abide.

an imperfect world

The Republicans are out in force, with the Royalists
yapping like terriers at their heels.
All this argument about it and about
What does it do for our country, anyway?
Will the grass grow any faster in the drought?
And the crops be more abundant, or the cattle fatter
because we are one, or the other?
Queues of jobless, lining up for the dole – what do they care?

My country right or wrong.
Do we really still say that?
Is Nationalism still a towering force,
Or are we at last beginning to perceive that we are indeed citizens of the world?
Truth and justice – abstracts both -
How nice if they finally had a touch of reality about them
but wait – don't expect too much.
This is a very imperfect world we live in.

And who shall take care of the children?
The concrete pavements of the street cry out
'Why are we beds for the youth of this generation.
Surely the caves of old would be warmer and more comfortable?'
Have we then regressed so far?
Cry out, you children of today,
Cry out against the farm being wrought you.
Save the children of tomorrow from your fate, or worse.
Go tell the people, tell them how so many of you fare,
Living your half-lives of misery and near-starvation
In this nether-world you inhabit
How you spend your days and nights in the streets of this lucky country.

Make your voices heard – do not go quietly to the grave
with your questions still unanswered, your lives unlived,
And your deaths mourned by no one.
Cry aloud – make your voices heard
That men of goodwill might hear.
We thank God there are still men of good will to hear.

We cannot let out heritage turn to ashes while argument rages on,
This is our country.
This is the land we love.
We need to be able to hold our heads high and say
'We have done our best for all our citizens.
We are our own nation,
We can indeed hold up our heads
As members of the human race.'

From a Hospital Bed

Night -
And the streets glare.
A thousand watts beaming out to light the darkness.
A car speeds past – horn blaring -
careless of others.
The flag outside my window, at full stretch all day
in the blustery wind
Hangs limply from the flagpole.

On a park bench, across the way, covered I newspaper,
Lies a vagrant – a young man – victim of the times.
A cat tries to join him – seeking company -
only to be roughly pushed aside.
He wants no company – human or animal.

A siren blasts the air – screaming in pain on its mission of mercy.
Silence descends once more,
Save for the soft thud of shoes in the corridor.
Night noises, muffled in the dark.
Soft murmurs of voices in the distance.
The quiet is almost unnerving.
Only I seem to be awake in this whispering
world of pain and suffering.
Tomorrow perhaps I too will sleep like the rest.

Morning -
Darkness still.
A thin line of brilliant colour stretches along the horizon.
Last night's lights still glow brightly.
Slowly the brilliance fades, giving way to light.
Shapes and forms emerge from the darkness.
The lights go out.
The soft morning light takes over.
The flag stirs once more in the soft breeze.
Day has arrived.

Trolleys with steaming cups of tea
Rattle outside my room.
Briskness comes with the morning.
Water running, teeth being brushed, faces washed.
A new day has arrived.
What will it bring? I wonder.

Cat's Meat

Down to the pet-food shop I drive
In the comfort of my car
And chat to friends when I arrive -
Their meat is better by far
Than the opposition down the road
though it's all fresh in daily
And besides they help me with my load
Which can be very weighty.

Twenty kilos of meat I buy
A mixture of three kinds.
Just so my cats have variety
I know that they won't mind.
Then off to my friendly butcher
To buy some for myself.
He gives me the very choicest cuts -
Right of the top shelf.

Thank God I live in Australia,
For it's very plain to me
We are still the Lucky Country
Bad as some things may be.
Do you ever wonder what you would eat
If Russia was your home?
And you queued for hours for some scraps of meat
And maybe a hunk of bone?
There you would find my cat meat
In pride of place upon your table.
A veritable feast for all.
Count your blessings, while you are able.

I Love

Cuddly babies, so warm and snug,
Playful kittens cavorting on the rug – I love

A gold day, shining and blue,
A mountain-top with a breathtaking view – I love

Strains of a glorious symphony,
A young child laughing on her father's knee – I love

The delicious aroma of fresh-baked bread,
A sad-eyed clown, standing on his head – I love

A letter from a friend now far away,
Lilting music, so bright and gay – I love

Birdsong at evening when all is still,
Your hand in mine as we climb the hill – I love

But most of all because you are you, you – I love.

Melbourne Seasons

Spring

Softly and slowly you stole into my life
Singing of love and laughter,
Of bees buzzing in the pear tree,
Of magpies carolling in the gums
Of roses blooming along the path
And baby birds in nests under the eaves,
Soft scents carried on the wind,
Sweet smell of lavender perfuming the air
the cold earth of winter silently stirring with a new warmth -
Spring, that life-giving season returns once more.

Summer

The day was hot and breathless
The air seemed scarcely to move
A hush hung over the earth -
even the birds ceased to chatter,
as if they too were waiting for something.
Then the north wind stirred in the trees -
Faintly at first, then stronger, carrying on it the smell
of leaves burning -
Stronger and stronger it blew, dropping burnt twigs in its wake.
The birds that had been silent were suddenly noisy -
Chirping and chattering, as they soared swiftly overhead.
The air thickened with smoke, cloying and smothering,
And out in the bush the flames leapt high.
Birds who were too slow to take off dropped as they flew,
Small animals and cattle died where they stood.
The terrible road hurried on, taking everything in its path.
The first days of summer had arrived.

Autumn

The colours of the world
How glorious they are!
I could scarcely believe what I was seeing -
I had known only summer and winter in Queensland

trees were always green, spreading their banner of shade
Hard blue skies and the sun always a golden yellow.
And in October, to my great delight
The wonderful mauve of the jacarandas.
How I loved them, and that marvellous carpet of colour
which formed beneath their spreading arms.

But this, this was something different
Something I had never imagined.
The wonderful warmth of the colours of autumn
Browns and yellows, reds and golds, trees aflame
with marvellous plumage,
Flaunting their beauty for all to see.

Winter

Trees, their branches bare, silhouetted against a sullen sky -
Grey light shedding its watery bleakness over all
Bitter winds biting through clothes
Piercing skin and flesh with icy chill -
Winter is here, breathing its clouds of vapour,
Plucking with frozen fingers at everything in its path.

Winter – the other side –
Season of log fires burning in the grate
Cold hands warmed to live before a cheery blaze
Curtains drawn against the greyness
Keeping in warmth and light.
The tempting smell of hot soup simmering on the stove,
The cat washing itself in its favourite spot before the fire
Hot chocolate, warming the body with its sweet richness,
Beyond the curtains.

Winter – the season of contrasts –
Lifeless branches raised to the sky –
Golden wattle aflame with colour and light.
The stark beauty of the landscape
set against leaden skies,
The soft greens of the native trees –
Gums, silky oak, lilly pilly
Outside – the raging cold
Inside – the cosy warmth
A season of contradictions.

But my heritage betrays me,
And winter is not my season.
I have lived too long in Queensland.
Its beauty is to me merely a harbinger of Spring –
The season of darkness
Ushering in the season of light.

Youth and Age

Young and in love – the magic of it all!
Eyes that sparkle, and feet that walk on air.
Young and in love – can anything match the wonder,
The warmth and the beauty of a world that looks so fair?

Old and in love – eyes that can still sparkle -
A heart that lurches joyfully when you came into my view,
Old and in love- made young again by laughter,
And love, and joy, and happiness at the very thought of you.

The Gulf War: January – February 1991

THE CORMORANTS

My stomach lurches
As the images flash once more on the screen.
I try to look away,
I cannot.
I want to cry out
Dear God what did they ever do -
These graceful, elegant creatures,
that we should condemn them to a slow
Lingering death,
Their feathers glued together,
Drowning in a sea of oil?

Cry Havoc

"We must declare war", the leaders say
Old men, who have lived their lives
Men, whose sons are too old, and grandsons too young to fight.
"We must declare war,
They must be taught a lesson.
Have they forgotten other wars and the lessons they taught?
Have they forgotten the bodies, piled like garbage,
stinking in the hot sun?
Have they forgotten the blood, the gaping holes
where intestines used to be?
And the flies, always the flies
Settling in their hundreds on the rotting corpses?
And the corpses, they were our young men -
Now young forever.
Where is their youth and their middle-age?
Where are their wives and children?
And the grandsons they will never have?
All rotting in the dung-heap with them,
their dreams and hopes and loves,
Finished before they began.
'They shalt not grow old'.
Oh, no! They will be forever young – forever mourned.
Lost to the world are the talents they might have had.
Lost, the ideals and ideas, their plans to shape a better world.
Lost in a desert, so far from home.
Lost amid an alien people.

And the leaders with their cries of
'they cannot do this to us – we must fight them'.
Where are they when the battle is raging?
Where are they when the bombs are falling?
Where are they when the flies are settling once more
on the faces of the young men.

'We must declare war'.
So long as others fight it for us.
'we must declare war'.
But do not ask us to lie, rotting and stinking
to lie with our stomachs ripped open
And covered with fliers
forever far from home.

a Beautiful World

I sit on the sand and gaze far out to the horizon.
The ocean, always my solace,
Lies deep and blue before me.
Waves hit the shore with a rhythmic clunk,
As seagulls swoop and dive,
Gracefully eluding the outstretched fingers of laughing children.
Here, all is tranquil.
The water sparkles gaily, with white-caps cheekily astride the waves.
Balm, indeed, for the spirit.

Then the picture changes.
I see instead another ocean
In another part of the world,
Dying. Choked to death with thick, black oil.
And all her lovely sea-creatures dying with her.
'How could we let it happen?'
Screams a voice inside my head.
I am sickened. I am angry. I am outraged.
Such a beautiful world has been given into our care
And we, may God forgive us,
Am not worthy of it.

Collateral Damage

The missiles rain down
with their deadly load
Some hit the target
and some just explode,
and blast into pieces
all in their way.
'Collateral damage'.
that's what they say.

But 'collateral damage'
Is somebody's wife,
and somebody's mother
Who's crippled for life
And children and babies
Now lying dead too -
They got in the way
As the missiles flew.

So when you read the news
With its cryptic view,
Be sure that you know
What it's saying to you
and what it's not saying -
for one thing is true,
'Collateral damage'
is flesh and blood too.

Desert Storm

An eerie silence envelopes the city,
The sirens have gone, the lights are out
The children, in their grotesque gasmasks, cower,
As the planes their obscene cargo fly overhead.
The world is once again at war,
And once again the universal insanity
Numbers as its first victims
the innocents of this world.
What do they know of oil and greed, of hatred?
Their world is being destroyed -
A destruction from which it may never recover.
Their future is going up in smoke.
If, in fact, they survive to have a future.
Chaos is reigning in a world gone mad.
Man's inhumanity to man has triumphed once more.

The War is Over

The war is over – why can I not rejoice?
The sound and the fury have ceased – the slaughter has ended.
Why can I not celebrate victory?
Is it the hundreds of thousands of young men, blown to bits among the tangled metal,
Their bodies unburied and littering the streets, that haunts me?
Bent, broken and smouldering buildings, in a city abandoned except for the human chaos -
The shattered remnants of a routed army, lying under shattered trees in a shattered city -
the corpses too numerous to count.
Machinery of war strewn uselessly in the way,
smashed, demolished.
Devastation complete.
We have won the war.
We are the good guys.
Why can I not rejoice?

SHAME

Dispossessed, homeless, hungry, cold
Outcasts in their own country
Abandoned by those who caused their plight -
Their children dying in their thousands
Their race headed for extinction
Human debris, washed up on an unfriendly shore.

Where are the nations who were so eager to fight?
Where is their eagerness now?
Where is their compassion for a nation no longer able to help itself?
Their token gestures are too little, too late.
Will their callousness return one day to haunt them,
As the voices of the dying children cry out for vengeance?

We have won the war.
But to our everlasting shame
We have lost the peace.

ONE SMALL CHILD

One small child on his mother's knee,
Bright eyes shining, the whole world to see
Healthy and happy – warm and well-fed,
then all snuggled up in his cosy bed.

One small child lying stiff and cold,
With a face that looks so very old
He died of hunger – he had no bed
Not even a tent to cover his head.

This one child multiplied a thousand times,
What did he die for? What were his crimes?
To belong to a race whose homeland is lost
Deserted by the world – it now pays the cost.

WHY?

There is sorrow abroad in the land:
Fear has gripped the hearts of the people.
They mourn the loss of innocence
They fear the carnage to come
they cry out against the pain and destruction being wrought.
They are helpless and hopeless.
What can they do to change the tide
As it sweeps mercilessly on, engulfing all in its way?
They did not want this war
With its potential for destroying the world.
They are terrified of the forces unleashed,
And powerless to stop them. Was there another way?
Where are the people who put a man on the moon?
Where are the minds who smashed the atom?
Where are the men whose giant intellects
Created these monsters of war?
Could they not use those intellects
To work for a peaceful solution?

I am confused. I am sick at heart.
I have no answers to give, only questions.
And my heart bleeds for the victims everywhere
For the innocent people who are caught up
In something they do not understand
Who must watch their children die
And never know the reason why

About the Author

Joy was born in Ipswich, Queensland in 1929 to a working class family. Growing up was hard for her family, and not made any easier by Second World War. In 1972 Joy moved to Melbourne where she worked as a clerk for the state bank. This is where she meet Ray, her lifelong partner and they were married soon after. Unfortunately Ray suffered from illness early in his life and died of cancer at the age of 43. Ray and Joy never had any children and Joy remained loyal to him until her death in 2007.

Many who knew Joy would have believed her greatest passion was for cats, given the number of cats she kept. However her true love was for birds, and she worked tirelessly in her garden to create a place for them to come. Joy always had a passion for English literature, particularly Australian turn of the century poetry. Her favourite poet and greatest inspiration was Australian poet, C.J. Dennis.

www.ingramcontent.com/pod-product-compliance
Lightning Source LLC
Chambersburg PA
CBHW070307010526
44107CB00056B/2519